WHAT'S NEXT:
2020 ONWARDS

PETER J DWYER

SWEETSPIRE LITERATURE
——— MANAGEMENT ———

CONTENTS

Introduction

The title of this short book is *What's Next?*, and the short answer is Who Knows? This is despite the mounting evidence that our current worldwide problems are leading people to reassess their priorities for the future and insist on the need for change.

There is a sharp contrast between what we have inherited as the priorities of the traditional state, namely "defense, public order, the prevention of epidemics and the aversion of mass discontent" (Judt, *Ill Fares the Land*, p. 78) and the emerging priorities revealed in a recent UN survey about "the world we want to create" which showed the global public's priorities were "protecting the environment, protecting human rights, less conflict, equal access to basic services, and zero discrimination." This kind of contrast has led one recent commentator to claim that, "a lot of people can't place the rapidly oscillating feelings they have right now: a rollercoaster mix of fear, sadness, boredom, tension and flatness."

The purpose of the book is to take this contrast seriously, and not only to accept the task of seeing what is at stake as we enter upon a new future, but also to face up to the challenge flowing from what this reveals: Can We Do It?

Obviously, the impact of the current global pandemic of Clovid 19 has had a significant impact on the text. It consists of twelve chapters, beginning with what I see as *Unfinished Business* in chapter 1, the main elements of *The Virus Response* in chapter 2, and what this reveals to us about what I have called *The Haunting Past* in chapter 3. I then move on to possible solutions, asking *Whose Responses?* in chapter 4, which examines the ways in which leadership becomes distorted as it becomes identified with dominance and the ambition of some to join the 'great men of history". Looking *Beyond Platitudes* becomes the theme in chapter 5, then the difficult question of *Can We Do It?* is faced In chapter 6, before bringing it all home to the immediate worldwide concern of *Is There A Post-Viral Recovery?* in chapter 7.

I hope that what emerges from all the evidence uncovered is some kind of viable future pathway that can help all peoples and their current leaders move on as genuine custodians of a safer and more sustainable planet for us all. Achieving this will depend greatly on the extent to which those who feel marginalised in our current world are included in the shaping of the future of us all, which is the main focus of the theme of *Active Voice* in chapter 8. Daring to take such an issue seriously forces us to go a few steps further. So, chapter 9 dares to confront the hidden challenge of *The Population Problem* and all it carries with it, before a further reflection on *Avoiding New Myths* in chapter 10 faces up to the myths about social change we always tend to carry with us into the future. The impact of all this on young people is the theme of chapter 11, titled *The New Adulthood*. The persistence of patriarchal dominance throughout the world provokes a final chapter, titled *Manpower*, but then the book tries to end on a positive note by turning to some poetry, even though it still cannot ignore the scope of the challenges confronting us at such a crucial time in the history of our species.

1. UNFINISHED BUSINESS

2020 was forecast by many pundits to be a year of recovery. Others seemed to be more preoccupied with what had become an on-going dilemma of human civilisation: are we making any genuine progress or are we just going around in circles? There appeared to be so much unfinished business, and even the very positive results of the UN 2020 survey for "the world we want to create" (protecting the environment, protecting human rights, less conflict, equal access to basic services, and zero discrimination) suggested the pundits were likely to be proved wrong, and then the possibilities of a shared concern for genuine change came from the mixed global responses to the corona virus, coupled with the death of George Floyd and the on-going racist problems related to Black Lives Matter.

With regard to the latter it should not surprise us to recall that the whole tradition of slavery coincides in human history with the formation of supposedly 'civilised societies', perhaps even as far back as 3500 BC in Mesopotamia. Later records from that Sumerian society identify a Code of Hammurabi related to slavery. It was common also in Roman society, and throughout the Middle Ages in European countries, followed by the Atlantic slave trade in the 1600s. Despite the American Civil War and the efforts of people like William Wilberforce in the UK, which led to the supposed abolition of slavery, forms of human trafficking still exist, affecting as many as 25-40 million people, mainly in Asia.

What recent events in the US highlight is the link between racism and official law enforcement attitudes and practices linked to notions of white supremacy associated with European colonialism of former times. For many protestors the statues tell it all! So, while we at least still honour the non- white male figures from the past (eg. Mahatma Gandhi, Nelson Mandella and Martin Luther King) who carried out actions for recognition and equality, the causes they promoted remain as part of our living history - or the circle of fate.

In fact, the circle of fate is highlighted by the profound implications of the George Floyd incident for American society. It reminds me of this reworking of a Time magazine cover I recently saw which draws a direct link between 1968 and 2015.

A mere 5 years later in 2020 we are once again reliving history and its circle of fate. Fortunately, this time fatalism is not the most popular response to our unfinished business, even though there are still accompanying outbreaks of extremism, like the despoiling of statues, that may lead some people to begin losing hope, and may even return us all to the age-old dualism of "us-v-them". For many of the protestors - and their critics - the statues tell it all!

The linking of statues and history brings me to the point at which I feel forced to repeat myself and start arguing about the meaning of Time, and what even "time-honoured" ancient statues and images can tell us. In the Introduction to my recent booklet *Facing 2030* I was led to say if we are to act, before it is 'too late', we need to think both backwards and forwards at the same time. Thinking of the past (history) should always inform attempts to predict the future (forecasting). This avoids the mistake of dealing with Time in a more linear fashion – as a kind of trajectory, like a Spatial journey from point A to point B, which tends to reduce Progress to a process of 'leaving the past behind'. Our climate and population problems are clearly directly connected with this dominant 'linear mindset'.

There is a further major insight here. It is that a Janus-like experience of Time helps people to be happy to live with and work towards a comprehensive resolution of unresolved dilemmas, whereas a more linear approach leads to resolutions of dilemmas by seeing them as an either/or challenge (*Facing 2030*, pp.3-4).

What this means is that even the statues, and what they represent to different people, are caught up in the mystery of it all. But there is also a lesson in that.

Some truth telling about it all is what is needed at this point in Time.

> Learning to live with diversity (and the mysteries it confronts us with) may be personally challenging, and may even be seen as a 'cop-out', but…… for genuine custodians, dealing with uncertain outcomes has always been accepted as part of the job. (*Facing 2030*, p.23).

It is therefore encouraging to note that many of the solutions already adopted to our current dilemmas certainly respond bravely to the challenges and so, while the challenges still remain, these responses can provide us with good grounds for maintaining our hope in the midst of uncertainty. So, even though we still often seem to be going around in circles in our attempts to deal with our common problems, we still display an ability to learn from our past as we face the future. Janus returns!

2. THE VIRUS RESPONSE

To add to the list of problems confronting us in 2020 onwards, our current global virus is undoubtedly a unique and extreme crisis that has caught many of us by surprise. At least some of the responses have been inspirational, with a global problem taken so seriously that it has forced me to reconsider the relevance of opinions I have previously expressed.

For example, in my reflection on Climate Change, which led to my new book *Facing 2030*, I puzzled about the mistakes we make when we are caught by surprise at what is happening in our world. I argued that in looking for solutions we need to avoid the temptation to come up with THE answer, because a sense of mystery is an ingrained habit of the real custodians of the planet. Because I had also argued that "thinking of the past (history) should always inform attempts to predict the future (forecasting)", I now am tempted to go one step further, and claim that it is important to be aware that such forecasting does not free us from maintaining our sense of mystery. For me this is one of the big lessons of the current pandemic.

The real challenge that confronts us now, therefore, might be to discover for ourselves how to balance two elements of the current crisis - scale and mystery, but with the caution that in doing so we need to avoid the very tempting solution of subordinating one to the other.

Unfortunately, many current responses around the world (by governments, the media, and even the general public) appear to have succumbed to that temptation: opting for the aspect of "scale" and even using it as a means of downplaying elements of "mystery". We are continually reminded that the pandemic is "unprecedented "and "exponential" in its effects, as if to explain away the mystery we are confronted with.

This immediately prompts me to remind myself of the importance of living with the uncertainty of it all. Because the scale of the pandemic is part of the mystery, we need to see it as part of "the uncertainty that mystery brings with it, and regard it as a challenge – not a disaster." As we scramble for effective answers, the big question remains: can we learn to live with uncertainty and thus avoid making the same mistake that so many have made before us: "that the only choice of moods we have is that between optimism and pessimism, when in fact the real choice we must face is that between hope and fatalism."

3. THE HAUNTING PAST

The human race has survived plenty of hard times over thousands of years. We actually thought we had reached a stage where the only problems we now faced were ones of our own making, like climate change and the diverse population pressures throughout the world. Then along comes the virus and it catches us by surprise because we thought it was none of our making. It looked as if the past was coming back to haunt us. Sadly enough, there was some truth in that!

There are many historical parallels which have two significant features in common: viral infections affecting whole populations of people, and an aspect of unexpectedness that caught both the carriers and their victims by surprise. Thus, apart from some frequent fatal outbreaks among native peoples during colonial invasions, there have certainly been widespread and persistent viral crises before, such as the infamous Black Death of the Middle Ages, which was largely confined to Europe, or the Spanish Flu which affected most of the world immediately after World War 1. In the 1940's there was an outbreak of the polio virus and then early this century the SARS virus made its way to about 30 different countries before being contained. It infected just over 8,000 people and killed 774 by 2003. Then there was the West African Ebola epidemic in late 2014, lasting about two and a half years, with more than 28,616 cases and 11,310 deaths.

The human race has been through it all before, but the current pandemic surpasses any historical parallels in both its scale and its mysteriousness. There is a vital clue in this.

Even when we turn back the pages of history we soon discover that the current pandemic is still very puzzling – while we might be able to find historical parallels they all fall short because our current crisis is so worldwide and yet so comprehensive. China reported the outbreak in late 2019 and official records showed that there were over a million cases by early April in 180 countries or territories and a death toll of over 51.000. One major trouble with the virus was that it could go undetected because the majority of infected people experienced only mild symptoms. The accumulated evidence now suggests that we can honestly say that we have seen nothing like it before, and that we will need to find some new answers to what might have seemed at first to be an old problem that we had previously faced and overcome.

As a first step, therefore, we need to make sure that we have the right mindset to find those answers.

However, even before we settle on a mindset, it is important to remind ourselves that history can still help us in other ways. For example, we can certainly find parallels in the ways previous civilisations made the mistake of taking it for granted that they were well and truly on top of things. Denials and conspiracy theories have been common reactions, but the concerted efforts to confront possible disasters that have also been successfully made have also often led to an air of invincibility and a refusal to learn from past events and own up to our human limitations.

In my memoir, *Life Journeys*, I reflected on my trips to Europe and the surprise I felt as I visited its historical sites.They revealed, in stunning monumental form, the triumphs and disasters of previous cultures and world powers — the Roman Empire, the dominance of the medieval Church, the splendour of the kingdom of France, and the reign of Napoleon.

The signs of unbounded ambition, deceptive domination and eventual collapse are there for all to see. There is so much we could learn from it all about our own limits. It all puts our pride in our own achievements into a much more realistic historical context. You begin to recognise that similar claims of invincibility have been made throughout human history, and you can see the direct physical evidence of superb human achievement on the one hand and our human folly, and even brutality, on the other.

A further problem arises nowadays on the economic front because of the claims that are made about the inevitability of the corporatist world vision. We ignore history at our own cost. Our visits to monuments, shrines, or museums are a constant reminder of once-mighty regimes that are long since gone. They are now the relics of history,simply because the supposedly all-powerful regimes collapsed, declined, were destroyed in some natural or man-made disaster,or overpowered in an uprising or invasion. None of them proved to have the inevitable command over human destiny that they had claimed for themselves. If one thing is inevitable, it is that the whole of history demonstrates that social systems, huge empires and whole civilisations are temporal. If we ignore that fact, we end up making the same mistake that so many have made before us: to regard our system and civilisation as if they are, because of our genius, everlasting (*Life Journeys*,102).

Still, the mood or mindset with which we react to our current fears and the fate of others around us is something like what happens with 'a death in the family'. Many people had told themselves that 2020 was going to be a much better year and now are full of mixed emotions, or as one commentator put it, "a lot of people can't place the rapidly oscillating feelings they have right now: a rollercoaster mix of fear, sadness, boredom, tension and flatness," The organised official policies about 'social distance" in public spaces poses a real dilemma for, and even a dramatic shift from, the mindset that has become so fundamental to our individualised culture - the need to "make your own choices in life" and "do your own thing". This tempts me to look for some answers in what I wrote recently in my book about another current problem, Climate Change, because its solutions also demand a dramatic shift from our prevailing mindset.

> One of the chief ways in which the current crisis affects us is that it complicates our lives. It introduces into our daily experience certain areas of conflict over which we have no direct control and concerning which all accepted solutions seem to fail. This does not mean, of course, that genuine solutions to social conflicts cannot actually be found, but it does mean that the eventual solutions will not be determined by simple 'local' actions but by the ways in which ordinary citizens respond to the much broader 'force of circumstances' (*Facing 2030*, p. 14).

Responses to official demands for ' social distancing' are many and varied as these contrasting scenes, in Spain and then Australia, of younger people relaxing together demonstrate.

4. WHOSE PRIORITIES?

Whenever we are confronted by the force of circumstances we have to find some way of facing up to our sense of priorities in life. We need to make sure for ourselves that we know what they are so that we can establish some kind of order in our lives. So, what are they and who determines them? To quote Tony Judt, "the priorities of the traditional state were defense, public order, the prevention of epidemics and the aversion of mass discontent" (*Ill Fares the Land*, p. 78). His list seems relevant today, but it is important to note that in response to the current pandemic not all countries have struck exactly the same balance. Big decisions must be made about whose priorities are the most appropriate.

For example, Italy and Spain have suffered badly because they did not give sufficient priority to the issue of 'public order', whereas those that have (such as Australia, Great Britain and America) are facing up to problems about how to handle 'the aversion of mass discontent'.

This suggests that the pandemic has exposed to the world that we are experiencing a period of Cultural Revolution in which competing sets of human values are in conflict with each other. What we are facing is a re-definition of the values people consider paramount and a re-ordering of the priorities that determine the way they organise their personal lives. At a more systematic level it involves a three-fold process: a critical analysis of the prevailing culture to discover its dehumanizing elements; concrete programs of action to lessen the personal and social costs that the prevailing culture demands; and thus to restore particular human values that have been sacrificed to enable that culture to prosper. (*Facing 2030*, p. 13).

I suppose, on the hopeful side, that we can comfort ourselves in the belief that there is nothing like a seemingly impossible challenge that brings out the best in us. This also means that we can still learn to live with our mistakes, even though it might take generations. Pardon the platitudes!

Another platitude we need to face up to currently, because of the magnitude of the problems confronting us, is the belief in the "great men of history".

How many can you name? For example, leading characters of Shakespearean dramas like Julius Caesar, or wartime heroes like Napoleon, De Gaulle, Stalin or Churchill, or national heroes like Chairman Mao, or Fidel Castro. There are contemporary contenders of course - think of Putin, Erdogan, Xi, Netanyahu, Kim Jong-un, or Trump, and so the list goes on. It is largely manpower, even though names like Joan of Arc, or the two Elizabeths of Great Britain, challenge the exclusive nature of the myth, as even do males like Lincoln, Gandhi, Mandela and Martin Luther King.

For me, the clue to this myth is that it is not so much about leadership as it is about "getting to the top". This brings to mind a strange experience at a conference in a college in Indonesia back in the 1970s (cf. Life Journeys, pp.43-4).

In the grounds of the college there was a monkey cage. Inside the cage there were two brown monkeys swinging on the branches of a small tree and a little brown dog. By all outward appearances the dog was used to the idea of being inside a cage with two very active brown monkeys. The monkeys, in fact, seem to have adopted the dog; they played with it; they stroked it; they cleaned fleas from its skin. Occasionally they even tried to teach it a monkey-trick or two; they would lift it up by a leg or by its tail in an obvious attempt to teach it how to climb the tree and swing from its branches. The dog did not like this, but apart from an occasional grunt or two, it put up with it. Just before the conference ended, somebody added a little black dog to the cage. The monkeys, of course, soon decided to adopt the black dog as well, but the dog resented this. Although it followed the example of the brown dog for a while, by the end of the day it had had enough. It began to whimper, then it growled, and finally it barked and barked right into the night. Eventually late at night, it won its freedom from the cage and began to run around the garden doing all those things, like smelling bushes and chasing insects, that little black dogs love to do.

The next day a strange thing happened. Perhaps the little brown dog had spent the night trying to make sense of it all and decided that it would never make it to the top of the tree anyway. It certainly seemed to have come to the conclusion that it had much more in common with the black dog than with the monkeys. And so, by about midday, it too began to bark. It continued to bark all through the afternoon, until it too gained its freedom. The little brown dog ran about the garden with the little black one doing all those things that little brown dogs love to do. The monkeys remained in the cage.

We were all taught a valuable lesson. Life in a cage cuts you off from what might be considered "normal" experiences. Ho Hum. Perhaps an even better way to understand the persistence of the myth (and avoid litigation from the great men currently in power) is to look at the life histories of recent "great men", (like Chairman Mao of China, or perhaps even Robert Mugabe of Zimbabwe and Donald Trump of the USA), and evaluate the transformations they undertook in getting to "the top of the tree."

To become so great they all definitely had to leave a lot behind. They proved to be somewhat exceptional in this and may have even regarded themselves as role-models, which partly explains the hierarchy that results from a patriarchal organisation of human society. The French learnt some valuable lessons from WW2, as the preserved ruins of the village of Oradour demonstrate. Over 300 buildings were systematically set on fire, and 642 people were wiped out. The ruined village has been preserved in the condition it was left in on June 10 1944. A simple sign on the old entrance to the village says "souviens-toi – remember." Other signs ask for a respectful silence once you are inside.

5. BEYOND PLATITUDES

The previous chapter was devoted to the issue of what priorities nowadays determine our choices in responding to the force of circumstances. Some of my answers seemed like platitudes and then I realised that there was another priority, not even mentioned, that currently tops them all. I had actually referred to it in a previous quote (*Life Journeys*, p.102) which claimed that "a further problem arises nowadays on the economic front because of the claims that are made about the inevitability of the corporatist world vision."

Inevitability - one of the oldest platitudes about the "human condition" - has been used time after time to justify or excuse a dominative world vision that serves to keep us in our place and not challenge the prevailing wisdom. Currently, it is the turn of global capitalism, or what Fukuyama, back in 1992, termed 'the end of history'. However, three years later in his new book (*Trust: Social Virtues and Creation of Prosperity*) he was ready to admit that it is false to think that economics can be easily separated from other cultural elements, because like so many other forces in our lives it relies on human trust.

This insight of his will serve us well in the current crisis because it will help us distinguish between genuine leadership and the salesmanship that is part and parcel of the dictates of contemporary economic ideals. As the UK leadership scholar, Keith Grint, would argue, if we are all affected by what is currently happening, what we need is leadership aimed at persuading the collective to take responsibility for collective problems, which means that leaders must ask difficult questions that disrupt established ways of thinking and acting, thus putting an end to the 'inevitability' of it all.

This hopefully will free us from a reliance on platitudes - even those that are used as legitimate justifications for sustaining our economic hopes and dreams. This will therefore take us one step further: to criticise global capitalism for its contribution to our current collective dilemmas. Dare we?

Would we be ready to accept the following utterances of Ian Verrinder, a contemporary Australian economic commentator?

> There's just one problem. Our entire system of economic production and social organisation is structured around profiteering. Seeking out gaps in the market and exploiting price anomalies are the everyday activities of anyone involved in any kind of trade, from shopkeepers and grocery wholesalers to money market high- flyers who trade synthetic derivatives of complex financial instruments.

At least this might help us to understand better the motivations (not of desperate individuals) but of those trying to profiteer from shortages in Spain of medical supplies and masks, estimated to be worth five million euros, or even in Australia the organised bands of hoarders raiding regional supermarkets in search of toilet paper and other essentials.

There was money to be made (of course, the number one priority), but then the official government reactions caused surprise when they displayed a rediscovery of another important element of economics (distribution) that had previously been discarded in the global pursuit of wealth. Despite the prevailing economic platitudes which emphasised the importance of competition and rewarded the urge to "get ahead of our fellows", governments suddenly jumped in and began instead to put the community first.

This not only helped the many citizens who had become desperate about their life circumstances, but it restored a basic dimension of human co-existence that had been pushed to one side by the promotion of neoliberalism from the 1970s onwards, with the effect of preventing the collective from taking responsibility for collective problems.

There was a fundamental message in this change: survival was no longer a matter of just "doing your own thing", but it depended on a shared acknowledgement that "we are all in this together". To cite Verrender again: "in the space of a few months, as a health pandemic has gripped the world, all our preconceived notions of economic management are being questioned". But we must never forget that there is more to life than this.

6. CAN WE DO IT?

The current pandemic has proven to us that survival is no longer a matter of just "doing your own thing", but that it depends on a shared acknowledgement that "we are all in this together". This has forced me to go back over my recent writings to find specific terms that could serve as sign posts for a successful journey "together" into our human future. Hence the following list.

> Aspects of Togetherness
> mystery
> balance
> uncertainty
> hope
> priorities
> trust
> leadership
> distribution
> community

Used as sign posts, these terms take us from the <u>mystery</u> facing us in the present to a rediscovery of a sense of <u>community</u> for the future. It all sounds so simple, but we still need to ask ourselves: can we do it?

This unfortunately was one of the most important questions we had to face in trying to make sense of the challenges before us in seeking to resolve current differences about the issue of climate change. It therefore now confronts us with a similar requirement to develop the kind of mindset needed to respond effectively to this problem as well. The text of *Facing 2030* provides some useful insights about what is needed by us all.

<u>Mindset Matters</u>
build on a sense of being 'custodians' of the planet (p.11)
acknowledge the 'mistaken paths' taken (p.11)
ability to listen to, and learn from, different voices (p. 22)
genuine custodians deal with uncertain outcomes (p. 23)
all elements of our planet are inter-connected (p. 29).

The persistent problems of climate change raised the question of how current styles of leadership throughout the world are likely to take into account mindset matters such as these. In *Facing 2030* I expressed some doubt about this, and even went as far as to assert that "leading politicians across the world are quick to dismiss current concerns as part of a 'climate hoax' being perpetrated nowadays" (p.18). However, because the deaths associated with this pandemic cannot be dismissed as a "hoax", leadership now demands more openness and consideration than those politicians are expert at. An awareness of this possible shift of perspective has led many political commentators to rethink their own economic opinions and challenge accepted beliefs about how the world functions. Even the famous neo-liberal author of *The End of History*, Francis Fukuyama, has continued to modify his views and has now even become critical of what he terms the "cognitive dissonance" of right-wing populism influencing American politics in 2020. This points to the third element of the <u>mindset matters</u> list, "the ability to listen to, and learn from, different voices" - a form of leadership defined in terms of its collective rather than dominative purpose. Where have our "grassroots" gone?

If you are on the receiving end, history at least offers you the means to see behind the mask and know what is really at stake. Even though the current corporate gurus may pretend otherwise, ordinary citizens can find strange confirmation from the long distant past for the current masquerade. Some very ancient records have a remarkably contemporary ring to them, like the old Roman, Petronius Arbiter, back in the reign of Nero in AD 60.

> I was to learn later in life that we tend to meet any new situation by reorganising; and a wonderful method it can be for creating the illusion of progress whileproducing confusion, inefficiency, and demoralisation.

So the double-talk of those in power is obviously not a late twenty-first century discovery but an age-old device which has often been used to mask a process of disempowerment. A recent example of this would be the calculating way whereby Donald Rumsfeld, as US Defence Secretary, sought to justify the invasion of Iraq by the US and its Anglo allies. With his usual command of words, he sorted out for us the mistaken reasons on which the Iraq campaign was based.

"The message is that there are known knowns: there are things that we know that we know. There are known unknowns: that is to say, there are things that we now know we don't know. But there are also unknown unknowns: there are things we do not know we don't know. And each year we discover a few more of those unknown unknowns."

Meanwhile the rest of us are apparently just marking time, waiting for the next turn of history and the chronicles of fate - apparently too ignorant to see behind the many public proclamations that are really just deceptive exercises in doublespeak. Thus, on the one hand, leading politicians and business leaders, along with many columnists, pretend to the high moral ground and choose their words in terms of noble-sounding principles and ethical concerns. On the other hand, they continue to pursue their discriminatory free market agenda, by playing upon people's self-interest in a way that heightens uncertainties, and even fears about personal fates. The leaders then begin to make reassuring noises, and so return to the high moral ground in the hope that they can again mask their appeals to blatant self-interest. Sadly, the problem with this process is that these appeals to self-interest play upon people's misconceptions about those they see as 'different', who seem to operate by a different set of 'unacceptable' values in life. This results in an air of discrimination rather than a genuine sense of common purpose.

Can we nevertheless find leaders who put the emphasis on collective outcomes rather than personal domination? If we look back in history, we can cite Martin Luther in the Middle Ages, and William Wilberforce and Amelia Pankhurst in Victorian times, then Mahatma Gandhi, Martin Luther King and Nelson Mandela. Of all these only Mandela was an "official" leader, but he differed from others in his position (like Robert Mugabe, or Mao) who used the demand for change to put themselves first instead of healing differences or, like Mandela, pursuing a goal of "truth and reconciliation" - which he did until his successors came on the scene. Thus true leaders stand out as exceptions because they highlight and symbolise all that the unknown masses have been struggling for over generations of time. Success comes because the substance of change has already been formed - the old saying about a great figure as 'the right person in the right place at the right time' is probably closer to the truth than the myth of the great as the 'makers' of history.(*Recovery*, p. 95).

Can we do it? - the struggle of ordinary people is certainly worth the effort, and some effective leaders may even learn to follow.

7. IS THERE A POST-VIRAL RECOVERY?

Once we think that we have at last survived all the puzzling upheavals resulting from the covid-19 take-over of our planet and its peoples, the major focus of national leaders will shift to a reshaping of our world for the future. This confronts us with an old dilemma - whether it can be done without ignoring the lessons of the past and thus creating new problems for ourselves. Can we do it - are there any guidelines to follow?

The first, and for me the most obvious, is finding an appropriate 'mindset' to avoid our in-built tendencies to consign issues about our future to the Too Hard Basket. The most beneficial mindset at this point of time is once again to see ourselves, genuinely, as 'custodians' of the planet.

The text of *Facing 2030* suggested that by adopting this type of perspective we would escape from a trap, hidden in the claim made by financial experts in this century, that humans are now the Masters of the Universe. The claim was clearly thrown into confusion by the covid-19 take-over, and once again reminded us that

> civilization is an experiment, a very recent way of life in the human career, and it has a habit of walking into what I am calling progress traps (Wright, *A Short History of Progress*, p. 108).

Facing 2030 also proposed that our current dilemmas proved that we have entered another period of Cultural Revolution in our history, which offered us the chance of actually learning from our past instead of simply repeating it. If there are definite similarities with the previous cultural upheavals that our predecessors actually survived, there may well be lessons to be drawn about how the human race managed to deal with the problems facing it. For a start, it involves a three-fold process:

> A critical analysis of the prevailing culture to discover its dehumanizing elements;

19

concrete programs of action to lessen the personal and social costs that the prevailing culture demands; and thus to restore human values that have been sacrificed to enable that culture to prosper.

Hence my question: *can we do it?* - which brings up another criticism of the prevailing "masters of the universe" mindset - our inability to admit to an element of uncertainty in how we face the future. In trying to design a new future for ourselves we need to face up to a likely contrast between a widely- accepted modern human assumption about rejecting the past and looking for a Golden Age, versus the proven value in former times of actually uniting to <u>learn</u> from the past – a sense of a living history. Instead of seeing it as a question of leaving the past behind, it becomes a matter of learning to live with mystery as we try to shape a future for ourselves.

For genuine custodians, dealing with uncertain outcomes has always been accepted as part of the job. *Facing 2030* consequently exposed the need we have for learning from Indigenous peoples of all lands, who are obviously traditional custodians of the planet. Their custodianship has been proven right by the events of Climate Change which have left the colonial 'powers-that-be" at a loss. There is therefore a big lesson to be learnt from what the Australian Aborigines know as the Dreaming: it is that all the elements of our planet are inter-connected. From their arrival they travelled over this new land and learnt how to respect it rather than exploit it as new research is now revealing.

Researchers from the Australian Research Council Centre of Excellence for Australian Biodiversity and Heritage (CABAH) have constructed complex, detailed computer models to analyse how the distant ancestors of the Aborigines would have arrived on what was then the supercontinent of Sahul – which joined modern Australia and New Guinea by a land bridge. The first humans to arrive in Australia, long before the while colonists, rapidly journeyed to every corner of the continent using ancient "superhighways", which the new detailed modelling has revealed.

There could have been as many as 6.5 million people across the continent but sadly after Europeans arrived, there were genocides and huge losses from diseases, coupled with a lack of effort in finding out true numbers. Nevertheless, once people arrived in Sahul they could have settled the entire continent in about 5000 years – very fast by the standards of early human movement around the globe. The tracks identified by the new research also correlated strongly with what we already know about the traditional "dreaming tracks" of First Nations people in various parts of the country.

Peter J Dwyer

20

What they all learnt from their journeying over this vast and strange land explains why, for the Indigenous, there is no such thing as <u>the</u> answer to the problems confronting us centuries later, because that is an attempt to dismiss the complexities of our world by being single-minded, and deceiving ourselves into thinking that we can come up with a <u>single</u> solution (cf. Pascoe, p. 166). Or, as *Sand Talk* tells us

Creation is in a constant state of motion, and we must move with it as the custodial species or we will damage the system and doom ourselves (2019, pp. 45-6)

For many of us the official responses to the pandemic might have confirmed this understanding of our place on earth. Although it may have diverged from what we had come to expect, it could be viewed as an emergency situation and therefore, 'out of the ordinary'. We had so quickly forgotten the lessons of the bushfires in Australia and their effects that it was commonly accepted that we could return to what we saw as 'life as usual'.

Perhaps that explains why so many of us were caught by surprise! Then along came the virus and reminded us all once again of the dangers involved in preventing the collective from taking responsibility for collective problems. Unfortunately, for some of us this all begins to sound so 'old hat' – a return to the 1970s and all those social scientists (from Alinsky, Bell and Drucker to Sennett, Simon and Toffler) who had become so preoccupied with what they called 'total society change'. At the time they were not alone in this. For example, the first 1971 issue of Time summed up the preceding year in a four-page spread of 47 pictures, which what was seen as the prevailing turmoil in all the traditional structures of society.

So, as we now look back with 50 years of hindsight we need not deceive ourselves about what the future holds for us. If you are on the receiving end, history at least offers you the means to see behind the mask and know what is really at stake. Remember what was quoted earlier from the old Roman, Petronius Arbiter, as far ago as the year AD 60?

> I was to learn later in life that we tend to meet any new situation by ; and a wonderful method it can be for creating the illusion of progress while producing confusion, inefficiency, and

The lessons of history suggest that we cannot ignore the fact that his age-old words offer us a timely reminder of one possible outcome to our current crisis – . There is a definite chance that, once we have 'cleared the decks', finding ways to return to the old order of things will resume top priority once all the 'emergency measures' are put on hold. Alongside those age-old words of Petronius, the age-old game of the power-brokers also persists and, as in the past, it might even be offered as a lasting source of amusement for all!

There is, however, another side to this story which leaves me with a further quote:

> Unfortunately we all too readily assume that to talk seriously of crisis is to indulge in pessimism, or that the only prophets that exist are prophets of doom. This is ultimately the most important dimension of crisis. It deludes us into thinking that the only choice of moods we have is that between optimism and pessimism, when in fact the real choice we must face is that between hope and fatalism. This has a fundamental bearing on the way we go about looking for answers (*Recovery*, p. 80).

And the answers are there. Lots of them. For example, recent social analysts (like Riane Eisler, the renowned author of *The Chalice and the Blade*, or Tony Judt and his final *Ill Fares the Land*), have provided substantial critiques of patriarchy and neo-liberalism. They may not as yet have provided the perfect solution welcomed by all, but together the rest of us can still build on their insights and begin the job of creating a new future. This will enable us to start on a mission that can carry us beyond the needless repetition of all those age-old attempts at which have all resulted in the sad perpetuation of widespread disempowerment!

So, let us start with the preliminary results of the UN 2020 survey of the global public's priorities for "the world we want to create". This is their agenda:

> protecting the environment,
> protecting human rights,
> less conflict,
> equal access to basic services, and
> zero discrimination.

A formidable list – but also, sadly, yet another public record of "unfinished business", which we discussed Chapter 1. There is still some hope left, however, because of the shift of consciousness demanded by the prevailing response to the pandemic. In America, for example, a dispute over the wearing of masks has highlighted a possible conflict between a concern for public safety and a belief in the need to maintain our personal liberty. This conflict brings with it a fundamental message for us all: survival is no longer a matter of just "doing your own thing", but it ultimately depends on a shared acknowledgement that "we are all in this together".

If so, this will bring us to the 3Cs of collective choice: complexity, comprehensiveness and, most importantly, consultation. All nations will have to contend with it all. Strange things will happen that will take us all out of our comfort zones.

8. ACTIVE VOICE

The previous chapter ends with three significant words: most importantly, consultation. What this next chapter is driven by is the awareness that genuine consultation is not just a matter of words but a genuine effort to learn from each other. It calls to mind the efforts of people like Paolo Friere to reach out to those often referred to as 'the marginalised', who are people not even seen as worthy of consideration. He advocated an interactive dialogue with the marginalised for the purpose of restoring active voice to people who felt that they had been excluded from any genuine participation or future in their own societies. He firmly believed that "cooperation can only be achieved through communication", and that the resultant dialogue with the marginalised "does not impose, does not manipulate, does not domesticate, does not "sloganise" (Freire, *Pedagogy of the Oppressed*, p. 168).

The recent experience of Americans during the Trump years provides evidence of the wisdom behind this insight and of the difference between genuine consultation and deceptive manipulation, and is a clear warning sign about how to take the marginailsed seriously in any likely discussion about our common futures. The insight also guards against the deceptive ways in which the first peoples of our planet have so frequently been treated by their domineering colonists, but, as Friere himself proved, it also guards us against cheap point-scoring in attempting to redress the errors of the past.

So, the challenge becomes much more than our differences but learning how to respect them and how to come up with a united view of the future that looks after each one of us and the planet to which we all belong. This is particularly important for members of the younger generation all over the world, who are becoming so marginalized by current circumstances that they are even ready to subscribe to radical action groups and a wide range of conspiracy theorists, who are only too willing to 'sloganise' as Friere so wisely warned us against half a century ago. It is important to keep on reminding ourselves that If people—whatever their age—feel marginalized some of them will seek to identify an enemy that they feel they can deal with or feel superior to, even if it means taking the law into their own hands. They find themselves living in a world that is unable to face up to the real-life challenges affecting all of our futures and on so many issues we seem to have gone backwards rather than forwards. The differences of opinion on the urgent issue of climate change forced me in *Facing 2030* (p.12) to wonder whether we are turning the clock back even further than we realise. I argued that we seem to be

> reverting to the old antipathies and simplistic dogmatisms of the Middle Ages, as each group or nation appeals to its particular god to justify its own inhumanity. A series of constraining dualisms confronts us, and some abstract predetermined slogan or principle is invoked to justify competing claims to what is true and right. You are meant to take sides.

That is why the wisdom of Paolo Friere seems as relevant today as it was some fifty years ago. He wrote of the need for a process of cultural synthesis between competing parties as the genuine means of resolving competing world views. Cultural synthesis accepts that differences of opinion exist: "indeed, it is based on these differences. It *does* deny the *invasion* of one by the other, but affirms the undeniable *support* each gives to the other (Freire, *Pedagogy of the Oppressed*, p. 183.) Even though the same old problems remain (which view must dominate and who must come out on top), there are still those who will not be deterred and will persist in seeking a new future that we can all share.

9. THE POPULATION PROBLEM

In my recent book, *Facing 2030*, I included an historical review titled *The Passage of Time* which included data on the enormous growth of the human population from about 1 million back in 10,000BC to a massive 7.7 billion as recently as 2019AD. This made me ask myself how do we make sense of the strange events associated with Climate Change? Then along came the covid19 pandemic, which confirmed for me that we need to admit to ourselves that "what happens as a result of the passage of Time is of immense importance to the future of all of us earthlings, even though in recent times we have become much more pre-occupied with the 'conquest' of Space, both on and off this wonderful planet of ours" (*Facing 2030* p.2).

In reflecting on this I began to realise that the size and domination of the human species had brought us to a moment in the history of our planet when these massive growth numbers demonstrated that climate change is not the only major problem affecting our world and that

It is possible, for example, that the figures contain a hidden message: that if we are to act, before it is 'too late', we need to think both backwards and forwards at the same time. Thinking of the past (history) should always inform attempts to predict the future (forecasting). This avoids the mistake of dealing with Time in a more linear fashion – as a kind of trajectory, like a Spatial journey from point A to point B, which tends to reduce Progress to a process of 'leaving the past behind'. Our climate and population problems are clearly directly connected with this dominant 'linear mindset' (*Facing 2030* p.3).

This led me to realise something else: that a Janus-like experience of Time helps people to be happy to live with and work towards a comprehensive resolution of unresolved dilemmas, whereas a more linear approach leads to resolutions of dilemmas by seeing them as an either/or challenge. This further insight raised again for me the lessons of the Dreaming of the First Peoples of Australia, and their ability to keep alive a sense of wonder or even mystery as they coped with the problems they faced in this strange land of theirs, seeing themselves as "custodians of the planet" (*Facing 2030* p.20) rather than adopting the "masters of the universe" mindset (*Facing 2030* p.24) of the colonial powers.

As I now look back on all this, the big lesson for me is that "all the elements of our planet are profoundly inter-connected" (*Facing 2030* p.29), and that, unfortunately the "population problem" has now become the really big one we all have to face now as Custodians, which will protect us from once again deceiving ourselves into thinking that we have now become smart enough to come up with THE answer which all other creatures on OUR planet will soon have to learn to live with!

This all sounds very simplistic, but if we look at the worrying diversity of recent reactions worldwide to the covid19 pandemic we have a very strong reminder of how much more simplistic the quest for a single solution really is, and that the "population problem" has come at a time which demonstrates how much is really at stake for all of us. Strangely enough, this has forced me to open up the Too Hard Basket and relearn what I thought I already knew.

> Once we open it up, the Too Hard Basket is likely to contain the missing clues we need. To do that, we will need to learn to live with the uncertainty that mystery brings with it, and regard it as a challenge – not a disaster. The big lesson from all this is that the first missing clue has now been revealed. It is that, for genuine custodians, dealing with uncertain outcomes has always been accepted as part of the job.

But it does not deter them from getting on with the job. (*Facing, 2030*, p. 23).

However, "getting on with the job" is not as easy as it seems for many people. For a start, we are constantly confronted in the media by a series of current concerns such as "more than 260 non- governmental organisations signed an open letter Tuesday (April 20) urging governments to donate $5.5 billion USD ($7.1 billion AUD) to prevent famine from reaching 34 million people in 2021" which even takes us beyond the Me Too Movement, Black Lives Matter, Refugees, Asylum Seekers, Civil Rights Protesters, Toxic Autocrats, etc.

Taking to the streets sometimes seems to many as the only alternative they have for "getting on with the job", but all too often the only response they get from those in authority is not leadership but a return to authoritarianism - think of events in Russia, Turkey, Israel, China and Myanmar for instance. These continual confrontations bring us back to the false choices that reflect one of the perpetual problems of supposedly "civilized society" - or, as I have argued elsewhere in page 4 of *Facing 2030*, an on-going "us versus them" mentality. So, there is nothing new about all this. It goes a long way back in the history of the human race. Initially it was manifested in confrontations with the Neanderthals, and the first available records we have from Mesopotamian society of 7000 years ago document the mentality clearly. It is also a major feature of the records of the major religions of the world, such as the early years of the founding of Islam, and, of course, the Christian Bible - in both the Old and New Testaments. Even if we limit ourselves to the history of the Roman Catholic Church, the documents of the Inquisition are shameless in recording the treatment of supposed heretics such as the Cathars of southern France (cf. Montaillou, 1978), whose cliff-face dwellings have now become major tourist attractions (such as Montsegur, where in 1244AD the village was destroyed and over 200 Cathars were burnt to death together, in the name of God) or Queribus, unbelievably high and unapproachable.

10. AVOIDING NEW MYTHS

As I look back through the historical records, it becomes impossible to avoid noticing how we have used our religious beliefs to discover and perpetuate recurring myths that enable us to live with the uncertainties of life on this incredible planet of ours. Even to raise this concern risks the accusation of heresy - something which is also well documented in the same historical records. So, this chapter is an attempt to address our current uncertainties without attempting to create new myths to carry ourselves into a new future. Before I begin, perhaps I should take a bit of advice from one of the First Peoples of the land of Australia. We need to keep in mind that

> Sustainability agents have a few simple operating guidelines, or rules if you like - connect, diversify, interact and adapt (*Sand Talk*,p.98)

These are complex guidelines, far-removed from a simple single answer which is always the starting- point for the formation of a myth, and if we were to follow these guidelines the first lesson we would begin to learn is that we must adjust to the uncertainty that complexity creates. This does not mean that identifiable problems do not exist (eg. climate change, toxic masculinity, over-population), but it advises us to avoid the urge to find THE one-and-only answer which excludes all other answers and condemns their proponents to the dust-heap of history. Easily said, so is this the next great myth that will save us all?

I doubt it, and this is why in my recent publications I have continually drawn attention to the shortcomings of a kind of tunnel vision that prevents us from learning from the past and prevents us looking to the past to inform our future. So, for me there are now six guidelines for avoiding new myths:

Connect
Diversity
Interact
Adapt
Complexity
Learning from the past

Putting all this together has led me to the conclusion that "none of us really knows what the future holds in store for us, but finally one thing is certain. As with any living species that is under threat of extinction because of internal disruption or external disharmony with its environment, the best chance of survival rests with those who are both capable of generating new energies within themselves and also are ready to adapt to the patterns of change transforming the world which sustains them" (*Recovery* p. 160).

Many well-known contemporary authors, like Naomi Klein and Bill Gates, have taken up the challenge on the issue of Climate Change, but the real sleeper remains the issue I have discussed briefly in the previous chapter - The Population Problem. Until we are prepared to face up to this in all its complexity (like the worldwide refugee crisis and ongoing child mortality rates, or mounting problems like urban sprawl or even tourism, protest movements, racial discrimination and resurgent autocracy), we are deceiving ourselves into thinking that we know it all! I must confess that I am not proposing this as MY answer, except that I am willing to acknowledge that the population problem cannot simply be pushed to one side, let alone completely ignored.

Perhaps some of the reactions to the jury verdict in the George Floyd murder case are an indication that some of the world's leaders are resisting the myth-making temptation because, as a result of their own experience in public life, they are aware that much more is at stake. US President Joe Biden and vice-president Kamala Harris both welcomed the verdict as a first step because there is so much more to be done, or in the words of Barack Obama "If we're being honest with ourselves, we know that true justice is about much more than a single verdict in a single trial." How very different this is from the myth-making associated with previous American murders in our own time (the Kennedy brothers and Martin Luther King), apart from the Christian, Muslim and Bhuddist religious heroes whose ancient shrines remain centres of worship to this day for their followers. There are genuine myths associated with all this worship, and it is now part of our human history, but avoiding new myths takes us one step further as we face the challenges of our own time on Planet Earth. What we have to admit for the sake of all of us is that the time for myth-making is past, and that learning how to cope otherwise with uncertain futures will come to us when we begin to take all the elements of the Population Problem seriously.

This may turn out to be an exercise in "trial and error", but it opens the door to a genuine transition into a shared human future on this planet. The fact is that the problem is so complex that it provides us with many starting-points, because different issues affect different people in different ways, and with different degrees of intensity but, as long as the problem is accepted as our No. 1 focus in our attempts to create a sustainable future for ourselves and our planet, we shall quickly learn it would be pointless to try to have recourse to new myths as a basis for lasting solutions.

If any doubt remains about how complex the problem is, all one needs to do is to research "population problems" in an internet search engine. What becomes clear is that there are so many confusing, dogmatic and contradictory views and so much reliance on different sets of statistics that it is no surprise that there is no consensus on the issue. However, the recourse to some kind of statistical "magic formula" which has become the basis of contemporary myth-making could act as a warning sign and send us all back to the drawing board to broading our understanding and accept the sheer complexity as an essential part of the problem. The statistics may then prove helpful after all.

11. A NEW ADULTHOOD

A New Adulthood faces young people today as a result of a range of social changes. Firstly, today's teenagers see their future work lives as filled with both promise and uncertainty. They believe in the value of technology, in the importance of being flexible, and in the need for specialisation; they also believe that they will change jobs frequently and change careers occasionally. The predictability of the past that promised certain guarantees for the future has been brought into question at the very time that they and their parents had been led to believe that this new generation's future was assured. In addition, one of the taken-for-granted assumptions shared by the parent generation, and underpinning the expectations and heavy investment many had placed in their children, was an ambition for 'upward social mobility'.

Traditional family roles have been transformed so that now both males and females need to negotiate for themselves, and between themselves, how to shape on-going relationships that transform those roles. So, at the level of personal ambition they now face new demands. However, if we try to make a list of those demands, the question of balance remains the most demanding challenge. Here are the five most demanding components.

1. Life as a Juggling Act.
2. The Technological Self.
3. Taking sides.
4. Living with complexity.
5. Accepting constraints on 'doing your own thing'.

Firstly, because traditional gender roles are now subject to challenge, young people of all kinds now find that becoming adult has become a bit of a juggling act. In particular, those in on-going relationships are aware that life can no longer be compartmentalised along gender lines. Each individual is faced with a broader range of adult responsibilities. So, at the level of personal ambition, it is not so much that they have rejected the heavy emphasis on upward social mobility derived from their parents, but that for them 'status' and 'achievement' need to be measured against 'breadth' of experience and a sense of balance between competing demands. The Me Too Movement has played a reinforcing role in this.

Secondly, modern technology maintains the mythical belief that we are still able to "live in a world of our own". The Selfie enables us to show that we belong any- and every-where, and if we fail to accept on-line dating, or are not enrolled in a social network like Facebook, Twitter or Instagram, we are too old-fashioned to belong in a post-modern world. Even computers are becoming things of the past, but we have found new means of transmission for the old trio of fun, drugs and music. On the down side, there are still things we now really have to fear: a. *scams* (unless we ourselves are so computer literate that we become the main perpetrators), or b. that we may soon be replaced by *robots* in all those activities (like work, artistic creativity. and even sexuality) that humans once thought they had a special claim to.

Thirdly, however, when we turn to what is often referred to as "the bigger picture", the failure of many of our current world leaders to face up to the challenges presented by major issues (suchas Black Lives Matter, Refugees, Asylum Seekers, and Cimate Change) has provoked many of the younger generation to feel that they have to take the law into their own hands. This is an issue I have discussed at length in previous writings (cf. *Facing 2030*, p.16), but it becomes a real matter for concern because of the failure of leadership. whereas even those of previous generations who joined protest movements had believed that they could rely on some genuine leadership from those in power. A belief in "direct action" comes to the surface which leads to a search for THE answer, which inevitably leaves many new adults feeling that they are now forced to 'take sides'. instead of learning to live with mystery, they become motivated by a feeling that pits one tribe against another.

Fourthly, however, in response to "the bigger picture", a respect for the complexity of our world seems to have re-surfaced. For the parent generation, one of the long-lasting outcomes of what was called The Age of Enlightenment was a belief that modern science had all the answers and to be "with it" we needed to know how to leave the past behind us, and leave it to religious beliefs to explain away whatever complexities or mysteries might remain. For many of the new adulthood, there remains the challenge of finding new ways of learning to live with mystery, which often means giving recognition to the First Peoples of our world who have sustained themselves over the centuries as Custodians of the Planet, rather than Masters of the Universe. What they all learnt from their journeying over vast and strange lands explains why, for the Indigenous, there is no such thing as <u>the</u> answer to the problems confronting us centuries later, because that is an attempt to dismiss the complexities of our world by being single-minded, and deceiving ourselves into thinking that we can come up with a <u>single</u> solution (cf. Pascoe, p. 166).

Fifthy, there is the persistent challenge of a need for a shift of mindset: realising that survival is no longer a matter of just "doing your own thing", but it depends on a shared acknowledgement that "we are all in this together". As future custodians of our planet many of the younger generation now feel forced to look beyond their own lives and pay attention to what is happening to their fellow human-beings, such as refugees, the victims of war, and the likely victims of climate change.

As someone born during the Depression of the 1930s, growing up during WW2, and participating in the protests of the 1960's, I too am faced by this New Adulthood. Of these 5 challenges, the final 2 in particular resonate with me: seeing ourselves as Custodians of the Planet, instead of Masters of the Universe; and sharing the acknowledgement that "we are all in this together". The two are summed up well for me by the Aboriginal author of *Sand Talk,* who tells us

> Creation is in a constant state of motion, and we must move with it as the custodial species or we will damage the system and doom ourselves (2019, pp. 45-6).

12. MANPOWER

One of the surviving myths of the human species is the belief in the great men of history. How many can you name? For example, leading characters of Shakespearean dramas like Julius Caesar, or wartime heroes like Napoleon or Churchill, or national heroes like Chairman Mao,. There are contemporary contenders of course - think of Putin, Erdogan, Xi. Netanyahu, Kim Jong-un, or Trump, and so the list goes on. It is largely manpower, even though names like Joan of Arc, or the two Elizabeths of Great Britain challenge the exclusive nature of the myth, as even do males like Gandhi, Mandela and Martin Luther King.

For me, the clue to this myth is that it is not so much about leadership as it is about "getting to the top". This brings to mind a strange experience at a conference in a college in Indonesia back in the 1970s.

In the grounds of the college there was a monkey cage. Inside the cage there were two brown monkeys swinging on the branches of a small tree and a little brown dog. By all outward appearances the dog was used to the idea of being inside a cage with two very active brown monkeys. The monkeys, in fact, seem to have adopted the dog; they played with it; they stroked it; they cleaned fleas from its skin. Occasionally they even tried to teach it a monkey-trick or two; they would lift it up by a leg or by its tail in an obvious attempt to teach it how to climb the tree and swing from its branches. The dog did not like this, but apart from an occasional grunt or two, it put up with it.

Just before the conference ended, somebody added a little black dog to the cage. The monkeys, of course, soon decided to adopt the black dog as well, but the dog resented this. Although it followed the example of the brown dog for a while, by the end of the day it had had enough. It began to whimper, then it growled, and finally it barked and barked right into the night. Eventually late at night, it won its freedom from the cage and began to run around the garden doing all those things, like smelling bushes and chasing insects, that little black dogs love to do.

The next day a strange thing happened. Perhaps the little brown dog had spent the night trying to make sense of it all and decided that it would never make it to the top of the tree anyway. It certainly seemed to have come to the conclusion that it had much more in common with the black dog than with the monkeys. And so, by about midday, it too began to bark. It continued to bark all through the afternoon, until it too gained its freedom. The little brown dog ran about the garden with the little black one doing all those things that little brown dogs love to do.

The monkeys remained in the cage.

And it is a bit of a cage which cuts you off from what might be considered "normal" experiences. Ho Hum. Perhaps an even better way to understand the persistence of the myth is to look at the life histories of recent "great men", (like Chairman Mao of China, or even Robert Mugabe of Zimbabwe, and Donald Trump of the USA), and evaluate the transformations they undertook in getting to "the top of the tree." To become so great they all definitely had to leave a lot behind. They prove themselves to be somewhat exceptional in this and may even regard themselves as role-models, which partly explains the hierarchy that results from a patriarchal organisation of human society. But it does not have to be this way, as the two little dogs taught us. Perhaps an attempt at a bit of poetry might help us to move on from a very prosaic life!

GO, GO, GO

The virus came and never went
Though many vaccines seemed heaven-sent
If only there was a simple cure
Which eased the risk and made us sure
That nothing could stop us humans now
Because all our experts had worked out how
We can continue to live our lives
Like bees returning to their hives
But free to fly and congregate
And not be mere victims of fate
Farewell to closures, drugs and things we hate
We are humans still, and it's go,go go
Though wiser instincts let us know
There is still some sense in No,No.No.

My final thought is not a nought
Even if the young are both on the go and saying no
But what it means we may never know
And even if we have recourse to history
As usual we may end up with mystery
So our choice is to avoid all the scheming
And look for lessons from the Dreaming.

BIBLIOGRAPHY

Dwyer, P.J (2020), *Facing 2030*, Balboa Press.
Dwyer, P.J (2010) L*ife Journeys*, Sid Harta.
Dwyer, P.J, (2010), *Recovery: Towards a New Future*, Sid Harta.
Eisler,R. (1988) *The Chalice and the Blade,*Harper & Rowe.
Friere P., (1970) *Pedagogy of the Oppressed*, Harper and Harper.
Judt, T. (2010), *Ill Fares The Land*, Allen Lane.
Le Roi Ladurie, E. (1978), *Montaillou*, Penguin Books.
Pascoe, B. (2014), *The Dark Emu*, Magabela Books.
White, R (2004) *A Short History of Progress*, Text Publishing.
Yunkaporta, T. (2019), *Sand Talk*, Text Publishing Co.

www.ingramcontent.com/pod-product-compliance
Lightning Source LLC
Chambersburg PA
CBHW061142030426
42335CB00002B/71